SOUTH COAST RAILWAYS ~

CHICHESTER

TO

PORTSMOUTH

Vic Mitchell and Keith Smith

First published 1984.

ISBN 0 906520 14 2.

© *Middleton Press, 1984.*

Phototypeset by   CitySet Ltd, Chichester.

Published by   Middleton Press
Easebourne Lane
Midhurst, West Sussex.
GU29 9AZ

Printed & bound by   Biddles Ltd.,
Guildford and Kings Lynn.

INDEX

GEOGRAPHICAL SETTING

The coastal plain slopes gently towards the sea and is mainly composed of clay. In pre-historic times, the sea level rose and flooded several wide valleys, giving rise to the extensive inland Harbours of Chichester, Langstone and Portsmouth. The entrance to the latter was easier to defend against enemies and the weather and in consequence has been the gateway to one of Britain's biggest Naval Establishments for many centuries. Until recent years, Portsmouth's growth as a commercial port had been stunted by the Naval presence but there has been no lack of growth in Portsmouth, or the nearby towns, in the fields of commerce and light industry. The population of Portsmouth was about 60,000 in 1840 and the area now has nearly a quarter of a million inhabitants.

ACKNOWLEDGMENTS

We would like to thank all those mentioned in the caption credits for the assistance we have received and also our gratitude goes to K. Dakin, Mrs. E. Fisk, C. Fry, Hampshire Library Service, M.J. Grainger, N. Langridge, Portsmouth City Records Office, R. Randell, R.C. Riley, K.C. Ricketts, N. Stanyon, R.W. Stevenson, C.E.C. Townsend, Mrs. E.M. Wallis, D. Wallis and our ever helpful wives.

(Railway Magazine).

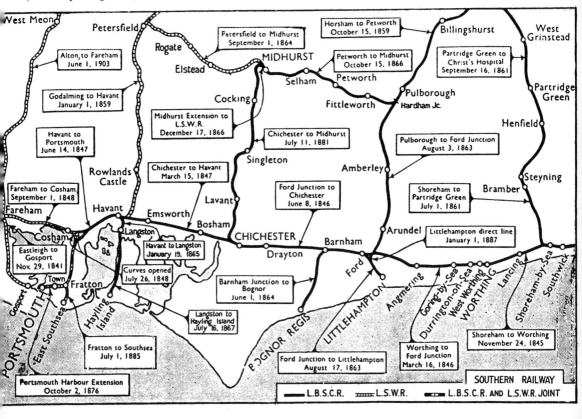

HISTORICAL BACKGROUND

The first railway in the area was a branch from the London - Southampton railway to Gosport, opened in 1841 by the London & South Western Railway. Portsmouth passengers had to suffer the double inconvenience of crossing the harbour entrance on the chain ferry and travelling through the town of Gosport, the terminal station being over ½ mile from the ferry. The lack of direct rail access put Portsmouth at a disadvantage with Southampton, particularly hampering its development as a port. The situation improved with the westward extension of the London, Brighton & South Coast Railway from Brighton to Portsmouth in 1847. The precise dates are shown on the map. It involved the penetration of the substantial military defences on the northern shore of Portsea Island and the provision of drawbridges. The LSWR had been planning its own direct line to Portsmouth from Fareham, but owing to financial difficulties and the £12,000 demanded by the Board of Ordnance for a further penetration of the defences, arrangements were made with the LBSCR for the line between Cosham and Portsmouth to be jointly owned. Thus from the Autumn of 1848, passengers from Portsmouth to London had the choice of two equally circuitous routes – via Brighton or via Eastleigh. Whilst this equitable arrangement suited the railway companies, it was not popular with the travelling public. By 1858, speculative builders had constructed an independent line between Godalming and Havant. The LSWR was the obvious customer but they were reluctant to use it for fear of antagonising the LBSCR. However, they were forced to lease it to prevent the South Eastern Railway from gaining control. The inevitable confrontation occurred, first in Court and then at Havant on 28th December 1858, when the LBSCR physically prevented a LSWR train proceeding by the removal of rails and the blocking of the line with an engine. This event has been over-dramatically described as the Battle of Havant (although one driver was forcibly ejected from his engine). Temporary bus services and further court actions were necessary before regular services commenced on 8th August 1859. The Chichester to Portsmouth

section had been built with double track but the direct line to London was single until 1878.

In the 1860s, extensions were laid to Portsmouth dockyard and to Southsea Pier, although the latter was a horse-worked street tramway. It later became the nucleus of the Corporation Tramwayss network.

In the mid 1860s, a railway was built southwards from Havant to Hayling Island. It is fully described and illustrated in our *Branch Line to Hayling.*.

The Portsmouth terminus had been built on the outside of the Inner Defences and it was to be nearly 30 years before those responsible for national security would accept that they were obsolete. Thus it was not until 2nd October 1876 that the one-mile extension to the Harbour station was opened by the joint Committee, bringing passenger trains, at last, to the berths of the Isle of Wight and Gosport ferries. To the south of the new terminus a branch was provided to the Gun Wharf and, to the north, a second line to the Dockyard was constructed.

The final development in the area took place on 1st July 1885 when a 1¼ mile long double-track branch from Fratton to Southsea was opened. The track was singled in 1903 and closed altogether in August 1914.

On 1st April 1906, "Motor Trains" (later known as push-pulls) were introduced between Chichester and Portsmouth, following their successful start in the previous year between Brighton and Worthing. New halts were opened for this service at Fishbourne, Nutbourne, Southbourne and Bedhampton but Warblington did not appear until publication of the 1907 timetable.

Electric trains commenced running on the direct route to London on 4th July 1937 and on the route via Chichester on 3rd July 1938.

2nd - CHEAP DAY	CHEAP DAY - 2nd
Havant to **HAYLING ISLAND**	Hayling Island to **HAVANT**
(S)	(S)
For conditions see over	For conditions see over

0330

0330

PASSENGER SERVICES

When the line was extended to Havant, it was generously provided with seven trains on weekdays and three on Sundays, all calling at both intermediate stations. The early Portsmouth timetable consisted of only five weekday and three Sunday services, with connections at Brighton for London. In 1869, the first weekday down train arrived leisurely in Portsmouth at 10.38 am. There were three other trains from Brighton and three from London via Horsham. The 1896 timetable showed 15 journeys between Chichester and Portsmouth on weekdays and five on Sundays, with the Harbour station omitted for early departures and late arrivals. The frequency was further increased in 1906 with the introduction of Motor Trains (one- or two-coach push-pull trains), starting at Chichester and calling at the new- halts (which have recently been designated stations). They made eight trips on weekdays and six on Sundays, terminating at Portsmouth & Southsea.

The 1924 weekday morning departure list from Portsmouth & Southsea gives an impression of the service pattern in that decade:

6.30 Victoria via Hove (Pullman Breakfast Car from Bognor added at Barnham
6.54 Victoria via Horsham
7.20 London Bridge
7.58 Victoria
8.16 Bognor
9.15 Brighton slow
9.54 Brighton fast
10.29 Victoria
11.35 Brighton slow
12.10 Brighton (carriages from Bournemouth West attached at Havant)

In addition, there were four Motor Trains to Chichester during the morning.

Electrification brought a speedy and frequent regular-interval service. The basic hourly pattern of departures from Portsmouth was one slow train to Brighton; one fast train to Victoria; one slow train to Chichester and one fast train to Brighton. This arrangement lasted almost thirty years, when what was still known as "The Chichester Motor" was withdrawn. Three trains per hour still operate, although the regular Victoria service was diverted via Hove in May 1984.

The development of passenger services on the Guildford and Fareham lines will be discussed in future publications, as only small parts of those routes are within the area covered by this album.

The through services from the South Coast to the West of England and South Wales are described in the *Brighton to Worthing* and *Worthing to Chichester* albums in this series. Their decline reached its lowest point when they temporarily ceased during the winter of 1971-72. During this period an afternoon local trip between Havant and Fareham was made by a DEMU, for mysterious legal reasons concerning the use of the northern part of the triangular junction by passenger trains. The revived services now include a train to Cardiff on every weekday and to Penzance on Fridays and Saturdays. Improved links with Gatwick Airport include an obscure overnight service from Manchester to Poole, calling at Havant at 5.52 on Saturday mornings.

London Brighton & South Coast Railway.

Shoreham-by-Sea to

Emsworth

BRITISH RAILWAYS
SOUTHERN REGION

MOTOR RACING AT GOODWOOD

EASTER MONDAY, APRIL 10th
WHIT SATURDAY, MAY 27th

Cheap Tickets To CHICHESTER

BY ALL TRAINS

FROM	Return Fares, Third Class	FROM	Return Fares, Third Class	FROM	Return Fares, Third Class
	s. d.		s. d.		s. d.
ALDRINGTON	5/7	GODALMING	8/6	PORTSM'TH & SOUTHSEA	3/4
AMBERLEY	3/1	GORING-BY-SEA	3/3	PORTSMOUTH HARBOUR	3/6
ANGMERING	2/9	GOSPORT	5/-	PRESTON PARK	5/11
ARUNDEL	2/8	HAMBLE HALT	5/6	PRIVETT	7/6
BARNHAM	1/4	HASLEMERE	6/9	PULBOROUGH	4/2
BAYNARDS	7/6	HASSOCKS	7/3	REDBRIDGE	7/6
BEDHAMPTON HALT	2/3	HAVANT	1/11	ROGATE	5/3
BILLINGSHURST	5/2	HAYLING ISLAND	3/-	ROMSEY	7/9
BITTERNE	5/-	HENFIELD	6/4	ROWLANDS CASTLE	2/5
BOGNOR REGIS	2/1	NILSEA HALT	3/9	RUDGWICK	8/-
BOSHAM	-/8	HOLLAND ROAD HALT	5/8	SELHAM	5/9
BOTLEY	5/-	HOLMWOOD	8/3	SHAWFORD	7/-
BRAMBER	-/8	HORSHAM	6/4	SHOLING	6/6
BRIGHTON	5/11	HOVE	5/8	SHOREHAM-BY-SEA	4/9
BURGESS HILL	7/6	IFIELD	7/9	SLINFOLD	6/4
BURSLEDON	5/3	LANCING	4/3	SOUTHAMPTON CENTRAL	7/-
CHANDLERS FORD	6/9	LEWES	7/9	SOUTH'TON TERMINUS	7/-
CHRISTS HOSPITAL	6/1	LIPHOOK	6/3	SOUTHBOURNE HALT	1/3
COSHAM	3/6	LISS	5/-	SOUTHWATER	6/6
CRAWLEY	8/-	LITTLEHAMPTON	2/4	SOUTHWICK	5/-
DROXFORD	6/7	LITTLEHAVEN HALT	6/10	STEYNING	5/8
DURRINGTON-ON-SEA	3/4	LONDON ROAD (Brighton)	6/1	SWANWICK	4/9
EASTLEIGH	6/3	MIDHURST	4/3	SWAYTHLING	6/9
EAST WORTHING HALT	3/11	MILFORD	8/-	THREE BRIDGES	8/3
ELSTED	5/9	MILLBROOK	7/3	TOTTON	7/9
EMSWORTH	1/6	NETLEY	5/9	WARBLINGTON HALT	1/10
FALMER	6/9	NORTHAM	6/9	WARNHAM	7/-
FAREHAM	4/-	NORTH HAYLING	2/6	WEST GRINSTEAD	6/9
FAY GATE	7/6	NURSLING	8/-	WEST MEON	6/9
FISHBOURNE HALT	-/4	NUTBOURNE HALT	1/-	WEST WORTHING	3/6
FISHERSGATE HALT	5/2	OCKLEY	8/-	WICKHAM	5/-
FITTLEWORTH	4/6	PARTRIDGE GREEN	6/9	WINCHESTER	7/9
FORD (SUSSEX)	1/11	PETERSFIELD	4/3	WITLEY	7/9
FORT BROCKHURST	4/9	PETWORTH	5/3	WIVELSFIELD	7/9
FRATTON	3/3	PORTCHESTER	4/-	WOOLSTON	6/3
GLYNDE	8/3	PORTSLADE & WEST HOVE	5/4	WORTHING CENTRAL	3/9

→ **RETURN BY ANY TRAIN SAME DAY** ←

For particulars of other reduced fare facilities from certain of these Stations :—
See separate announcements.

(1950)

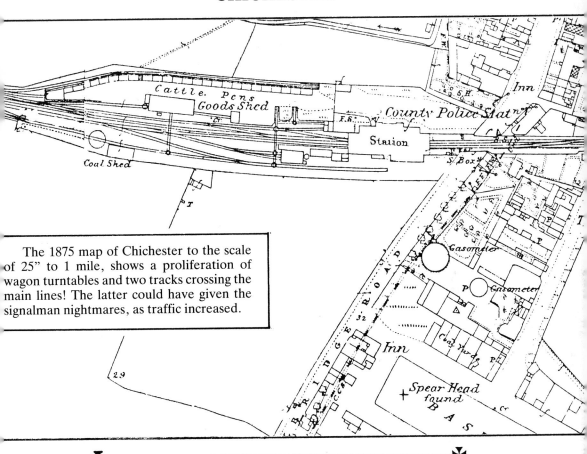

The 1875 map of Chichester to the scale of 25" to 1 mile, shows a proliferation of wagon turntables and two tracks crossing the main lines! The latter could have given the signalman nightmares, as traffic increased.

1. We commence this survey of the LBSCR's West Coast line with this well known but exceptionally good quality view of a Portsmouth-bound Express, waiting at the down starting signals. The wagon tarpaulins appear to be covering hay or straw, an impor-

tant railway traffic in the pre-motoring era. *Rastrick*, a well groomed member of the B2 class, stands by the nameboard which looks like a contemporary bed-head, with its ornate knobs. (Lens of Sutton)

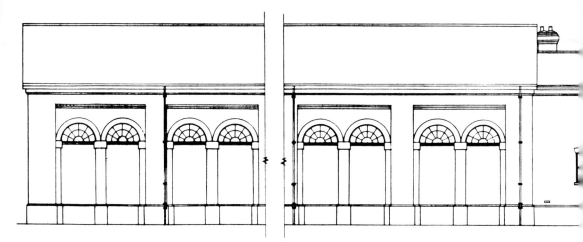

The goods shed survives today in commercial use and consists of nine similar panels on the south side and four road vehicle doorways on the north side. The drawings are by J. Brooker to the scale 2mm to 1 foot and continue overleaf.

2. G class single no. 344 *Hurstmonceaux* stands in the up sidings by the bi-directional signals near Westgate Fields, having worked a Goodwood Race Special. The stock is of the six-wheeled type, later favoured by holiday home builders on the nearby coast. (E.R. Lacey collection)

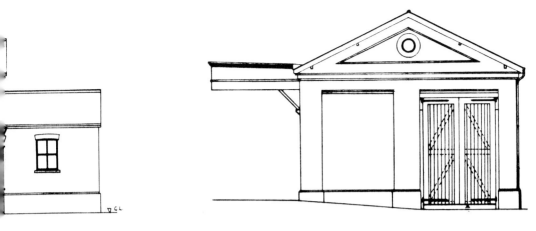

3. Being a railwayman can be more than just a job. The team spirit spreads into recreational activities, as illustrated by this 1920 photograph of the Chichester Railway Athletic Club. Note the hair styles and, in particular, the centre parting. (E. Godfrey)

4. A snap, taken through the lattice ironwork of the footbridge at the east end of the station, of a chore often over-looked or ignored by passengers at the time. Now, crowds gather at the platform ends on preserved steam railways to watch the fireman clamber over the coal to hold the bag of the water crane in position. The small wheel at the top of the column ran on an inclined plane. This prevented the pipe accidentally swinging onto passing trains. (E. Jackson)

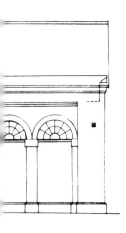
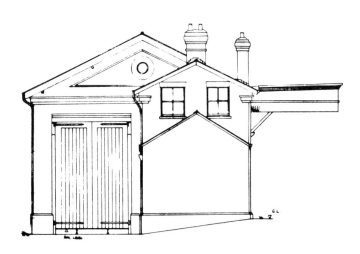

5. Another view taken just prior to electrification and showing the small coal stage which could be used by shunting locomotives or the engine operating the Motor Train from the down bay platform to Portsmouth. A connection to the Selsey Tramway had been provided at the location and is illustrated in our *Branch Line to Selsey*. (E. Jackson)

6. Sidings on the up side gradually en-croached on Westgate Fields and one of them was electrified to allow the Southern Rail-way's electric locomotive CCI to work goods trains. This 1951 view from the footbridge shows class C3 no. 32303 propelling a brake van onto its train, a few months before it was withdrawn. (C.R.L. Coles)

London Brighton and South Coast Railway.

Heathfield to

Chichester

8. Nearest the camera, on 7th July 1960, is no. 2066, one of two 2-BIL sets ready to depart for Portsmouth & Southsea, calling at all stations and halts. The re-building was complete apart from the canopy extension and new lamp standards. The barrow bears boxes of cut flowers, still an important traffic from local nurseries. (British Rail)

→

7. This photograph captures the atmosphere of the antiquated gaslit station, not long before rebuilding started. Note how low the platforms were; the luggage label rack on the wall of the *Gents* and the gap in the conductor rail over the metal roof of the subway. The latter caused inexperienced passengers in eastbound 2-coach electrics to be unexpectedly jolted and deprived of illumination as the other collector shoe was isolated on the level crossing. The momentum of the train eventually reconnected the supply.
(A.A.F. Bell)

9. Another transitional view, showing the temporary booking office and the East signal box. The latter survived until 1973, when the level crossing gates were replaced by lifting barriers. The water tank on the sky-line was built for locomotive water supply but lasted until 1983, as it also supplied the station's needs. (C. Attwell collection)

10. The mid-day sun on 11th March 1961, reveals the detail (and also the grime) of N class no. 31410. The class O8 diesel shunter is almost obscured. The line curving away towards the cathedral was part of a triangle laid down for turning modern goods engines too long for the 45ft. turntable, which was later scrapped. The third side of the triangle is largely concealed by steam and vegetation. (R. Holder)

11. Milepost 28¾ (from Brighton) stands at the foot of the steps to the former West Box, once known as 'B' Box. It has 46 levers, only 22 of which are now in use. The goods yard is now virtually closed and the Tarmac gravel train is no longer stored there, although its former presence has given rise to an incorrect description "Aggregate Terminal" in a recent reference book. (J. Scrace)

Chichester Directory, Handbook and Almanac, 1889.

𝕷ondon 𝕭righton and 𝕾outh 𝕮oast 𝕽ailway.

—

MARKET TICKETS TO CHICHESTER

AT CHEAP RETURN FARES

EVERY WEDNESDAY.

FROM	BY TRAINS LEAVING AT					RETURN FARES.		
						1st.	2nd.	3rd.
	a.m.	a.m.	a.m.	a.m.	a.m.	s. d.	s. d.	s. d
PORTSMOUTH HAR.	..	7 0	..	9 50	11 30	2 8	2 2	1 8
PORTSMOUTH TOWN	..	7 5	9 0	9 55	11 35	2 8	2 2	1 8
SOUTHSEA	..	7 0	8 45	9 50	11 30	2 8	2 2	1 8
FRATTON	..	7 7	9 2	9 57	11 39	2 8	2 2	1 8
HAVANT	..	7 19	9 13	10 9	11 51	1 6	1 3	1 0

12. A hard-working class S15 has been signalled by Fishbourne Box (¾ mile west of Chichester) to enter the goods yard, on 27th April 1956. On the right, is the former branch to Midhurst which still carries a block-train of gravel hoppers as far as Lavant, on three days a week. The line is one of three included in our *Branch Lines to Midhurst*. (E. Gamblin)

13. Signalman George Watson hands over the single line token on 11th July 1981 to the driver of a 3-coach DEMU special to Lavant. This train ran several trips that day as part of the centenary celebrations of the opening of the line to Midhurst, organised by your authors. The train made over £300 profit for railway charities and a £1 walk permit for the rest of the route produced £700 for Christian Aid. (D. Dornom)

14. A high proportion of the Southern Region's 198 level crossings are on the South Coast lines. Many between Chichester and Havant are still worked directly by hand, with Resident Keepers at the less busy roads, living in adjacent cottages. Here we see Mrs. Ivy Walsh at work on 18th April 1984 at Clay Lane Crossing, with the newly renovated cottage in the background. (V. Mitchell)

15. The next crossing is at Salthill Road and is fully staffed on three shifts. The tiny booking office is manned on a single shift only. Mr. Dick Hurn is seen opening one gate, which is linked mechanically to the gate on the right. Notice how the red warning plate has been worn by the knuckles of successive bolt operators. (V. Mitchell)

Roman Palace

The Roman Palace at Fishbourne is the largest Roman residence yet found in Britain and was probably built around AD 70 for a local king. The remains of the north wing with many mosaic-floored rooms, corridors, courtyards, hypocausts and bath suite are housed inside a modern cover building. A reconstruction of a dining room shows what one room may have looked like c. AD 100.

17. Class Q1 no. C14 coupled to a Q class are about to rumble over Blackboy Lane crossing, with Fishbourne Halt just visible in the background. This photograph was taken during the final year of the Southern Railway's existence, 1947. The prefix C was used on this class of locomotive to indicate that it had three driving axles. (C.R.L. Coles)

16. Another recent view shows a 4VEP arriving with a stopping service to Brighton, whilst the ganger strides away with his 7lb. hammer on his shoulder. The assorted build-ings provide (from left to right) a waiting shelter, a staff toilet and a booking office. (J.A.M. Vaughan)

BOSHAM

18. Within four months of the opening of the line, the directors decided to close this station, for reasons of economy. The frustrated villagers had to content themselves with watching the trains pass by, until their station was re-opened in June 1849. (Lens of Sutton)

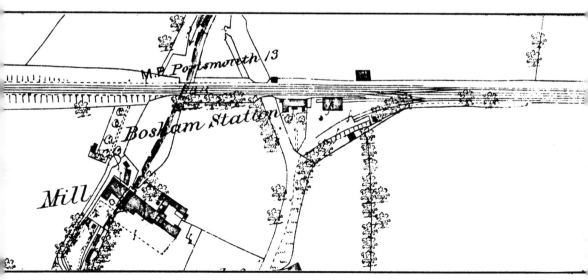

1875 map 25" scale

19. Their tiny country station was completely rebuilt in 1902-04, improving the amenities immensely. The platform height was doubled; generous canopies provided on both platforms; a larger goods shed built and the goods yard expanded – compare the maps. (M.G. Joly collection)

London Brighton and South Coast Railway

Mitcham Junction to

Bosham

1897 map 25" scale

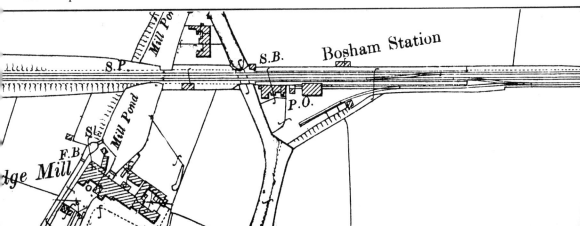

20. Class L12 no. 423 speeds past the goods yard with a train from the West of England, in 1947. In the distance are the white gates of Brooks Lane crossing, which crossed both the main lines and the goods head shunt. The inside bearing bogies gave a neat appearance to these 8-wheeled Drummond ("Water Cart") tenders. (C.R.L. Coles)

London Brighton & South Coast Railway.

St. Leonards, Warrior Square to

BOSHAM

1912 map 25" scale

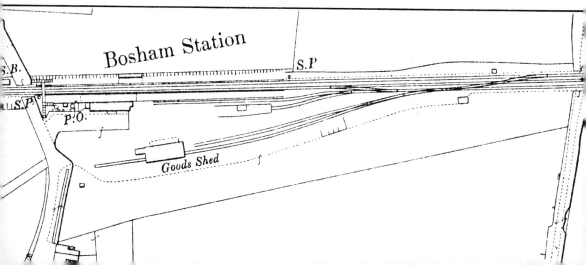

Bosham Station

21. The all-Pullman *Brighton Belle* was well away from its normal route to London, when chartered for a railtour by the RCTS on 8th April 1972. An elegant train in an elegant station. (J. Scrace)

22. The exterior elegance, recorded on the same day. The bold eaves and the mixture of elliptical and square window-heads, together with one circular light, gives a building worth preserving for posterity, even if it has to serve another function. Railway enterprise brought camping coaches into the goods yard in the 1950s. (J. Scrace)

23. The gentle arcs of the canopy complement the comforts provided for passengers. Toilets were even provided in this modest up platform building, although the *Gentlemens* sign has been lost. (J. Scrace)

24. The signal box has a limited life now that colour light signals and automatic lifting barriers are creeping westwards. This 1982 view may soon become history. (J. Scrace)

25. A view of all the facilities offered at the new Motor Train Halt of 1906. At least it was better than no trains at all. Most of the halts were built close to existing crossing keepers' cottages, as seen here. (Lens of Sutton)

26. The halts were all lengthened with the advent of electric trains in 1938 and most were rebuilt at the same time with concrete slab decking and supports. The booking office has lost its stove chimney as it is now heated by gas. Automatic half barriers replaced the gates in 1972. (Lens of Sutton)

EMSWORTH

29. A late Victorian view of an E4 class 0–6–2T on a westbound train before the platforms were extended. This extension, the alterations to the goods yard and the enlargement of the goods shed are evident when comparing the maps. (E.R. Lacey collection)

The 6" scale map from the 1870s shows the station to be separated from the town by fields. The weary traveller, upon arrival, had to choose between The Locomotive Inn and The Railway Tavern for refreshment.

SOUTHBOURNE

27. The presence of the halt has encouraged housing development, which in turn has generated more railway passengers, particularly to Portsmouth, the destination of the train seen in this picture. Note the SR concrete posts with hexagonal lamp shades. (P. Hay)

28. Modern platform and crossing illumination had arrived by 1974 but the ageing signal box and rail-built signal still stand today. Between this station and Emsworth, sidings were provided on the north side of the line for an aerodrome, during and after World War I. (E. Wilmshurst)

30. *Allen Sarle* was one of the successful "Gladstone" class 0-4-2s used for several decades on South Coast expresses. It is seen standing at the partially complete platform improvements and in front of the earlier signal box, just prior to its demolition. (Lens of Sutton)

1898 map 25" scale

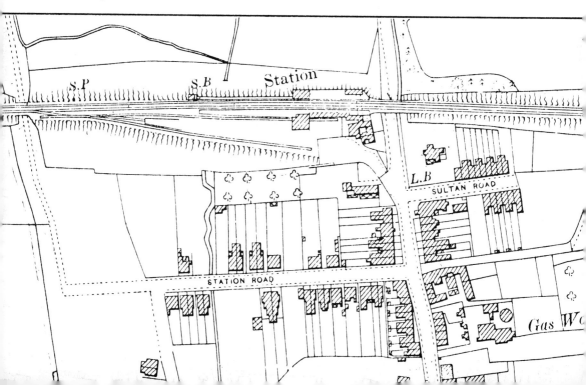

31. A small boy poses whilst this Edwardian post card view was taken. The down side buildings and the station house remain little altered today. (Lens of Sutton)

1932 map 25" scale

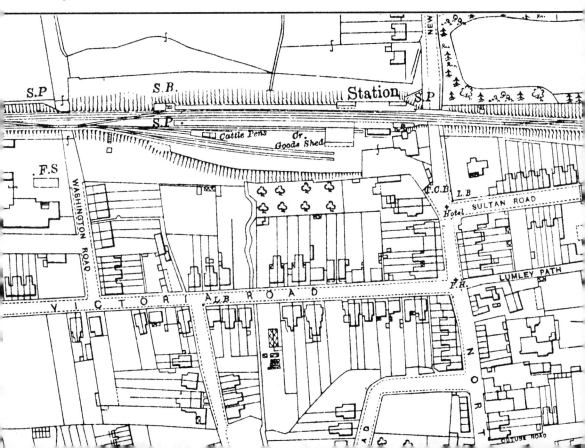

32. The new enlarged signal box had a worthy sign board, unlike the chipped enamel insult borne by its predecessor. A ground frame cabin was also provided. This still exists in a nearby lineside garden. (Lens of Sutton)

33. A once familiar part of the railway scene, before World War II, was the private owner wagon. This 1906 model was built by R.Y. Pickering & Co. Ltd. (HMRS)

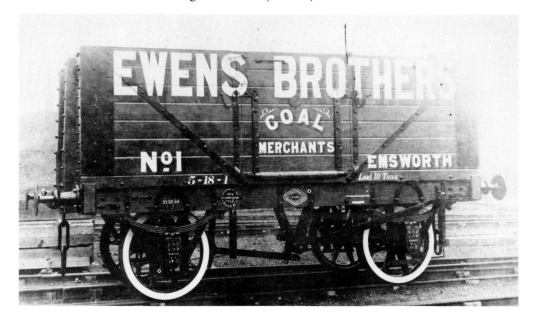

34. It is remarkable that this view of the approach to a wayside halt was once of sufficient interest to make it the subject of a commercially successful postcard. Note that the crossing keeper's cottage has been clad with slates to reduce internal damp.
(Lens of Sutton)

London Brighton & South Coast Railway.

Chelsea to

Chichester

35. This 1974 picture was taken four years before the gates and signal box were removed and replaced by barriers with closed circuit TV. Havant distant is located below the down starting signal and mirrors can be seen which enabled the signal man to see both directions along the highway, simultaneously, when operating the gates. (E. Wilmshurst)

36. Looking east in 1982, we see the cattle grids used to restrain pedestrians more often than animals and the usual minimal but functional buildings. The foot crossing is no longer used and the crossover has gone. (J. Scrace)

HAVANT

37. Looking eastwards between the low platforms of the original station, we notice the absence of a footbridge. This contribution to passenger safety was a latecomer on the railway scene. (National Railway Museum)

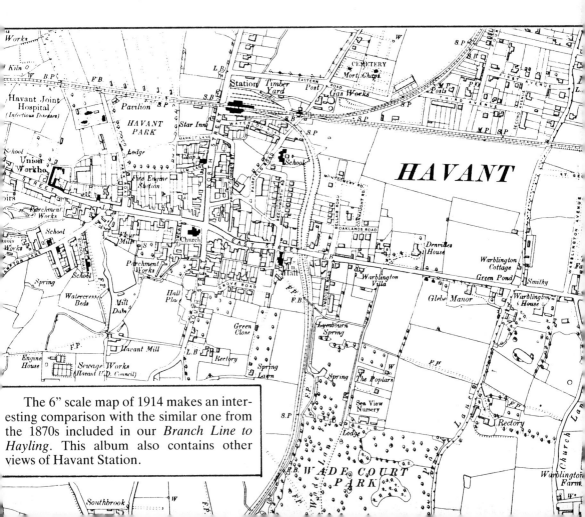

The 6" scale map of 1914 makes an interesting comparison with the similar one from the 1870s included in our *Branch Line to Hayling*. This album also contains other views of Havant Station.

38. Extensive rebuilding of the station to[o]
place around 1889 but the brick-built part [to]
the left of the rainwater down-pipe remain[s]
from the first structure. This March 19[??]
photograph was taken just prior to constru[c]-
tion of the third and present station.
(Railway Magazine)

39. The footbridge was, and is, an ideal location for railway photography. An LBSC train
is seen arriving from Chichester, around the
turn of the century, with the LSWR main line
and goods yard head shunt curving away to
the left. (Lens of Sutton)

40. Looking towards Portsmouth from the footbridge, we can see the level crossing wheel in the signal box. This was East Box; West Box was at the far end of the station whilst a third box was located on the LSWR line. The bay platform, on the left, was used by Hayling Island trains. (Lens of Sutton)

In 1938, East Box was extended from three to five sections; the other two boxes were closed and most semaphores were converted to colour lights. East Box, before extension, was drawn by J. Brooker.

Continued overleaf.

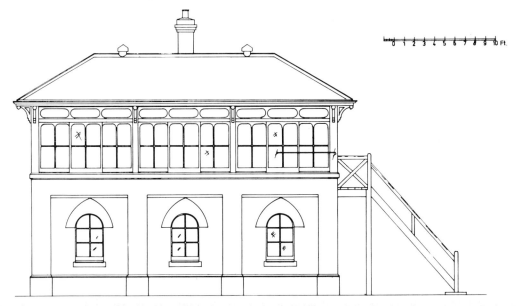

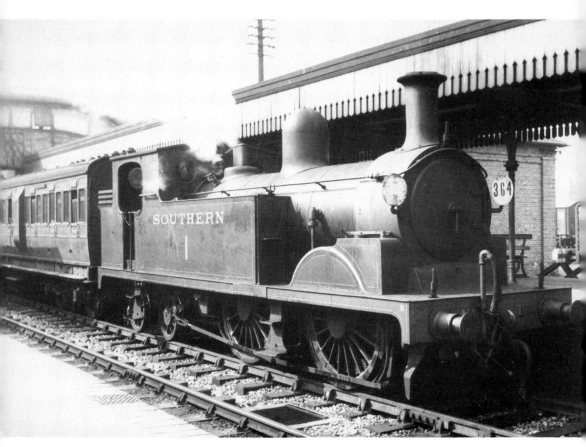

41. An ex-LSWR class T1, one of 50 built to Adams design, coupled to an ex-LSWR coach, one of a batch built with lavatories and unusual central guards compartments. This Fratton-based engine was normally station pilot at Portsmouth & Southsea in 1938. (C.R.L. Coles)

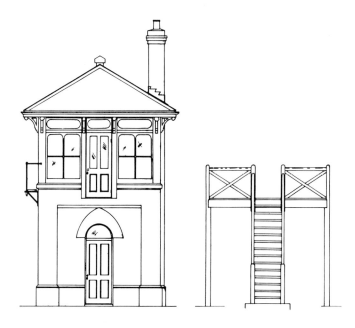

42. Once a common railway junction scene. The mighty express roars in beside the placid branch train. The date is 21st June 1936. The locomotives are Schools no. 928 *Stowe* (now resident on the Bluebell Railway) and Terrier No. 2661 (formerly *Sutton*). The latter was withdrawn in April 1963 and escaped preservation. (S.W. Baker)

SOUTHERN RAILWAY.

(7/45)
Stock 767

TO

HAVANT

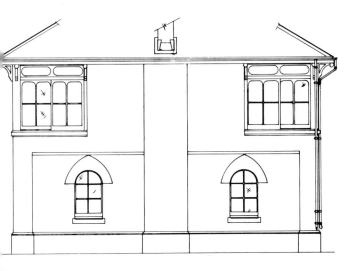

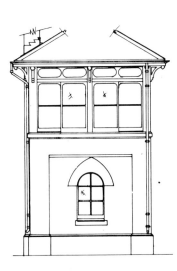

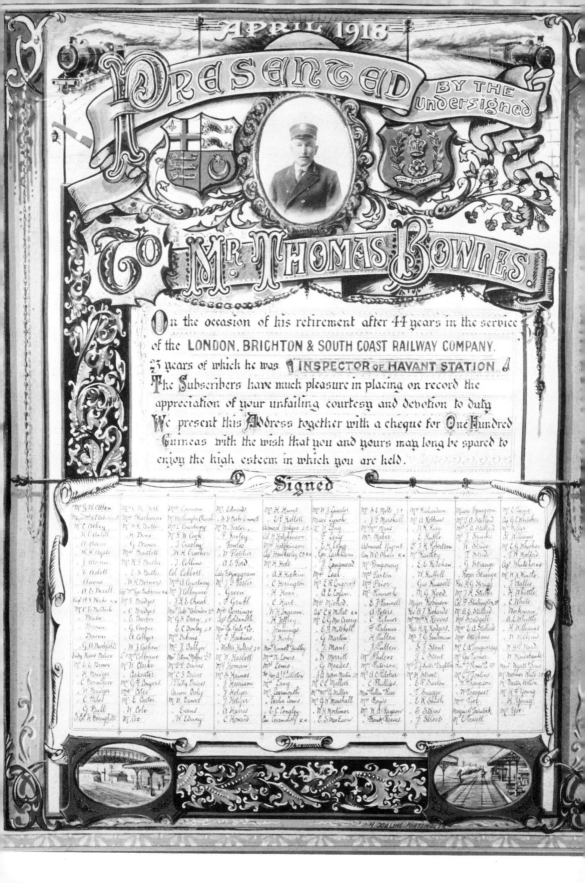

APRIL 1918

PRESENTED BY THE undersigned

TO Mr. THOMAS BOWLES.

On the occasion of his retirement after 44 years in the service of the **LONDON, BRIGHTON & SOUTH COAST RAILWAY COMPANY,** 23 years of which he was **INSPECTOR of HAVANT STATION** The Subscribers have much pleasure in placing on record the appreciation of your unfailing courtesy and devotion to duty We present this Address together with a cheque for One Hundred Guineas with the wish that you and yours may long be spared to enjoy the high esteem in which you are held.

Signed

44. One of the K class, fitted with a massive Weir pump for boiler water feed, pulls away from its short goods train to enter the goods yard, in December 1938. (C.R.L. Coles)

45. The west end of the new platforms (seen in the background) were brought into use first, enabling the old platforms to be demolished without closing the station. K class no. 2348 is seen on North Street crossing, with the roof of West Box just visible above the cab. (National Railway Museum)

46. A few months later, the new white platforms had reached the east end, roughly doubling the length of the original station. The temporary wooden platform on the left served the Hayling train, the temporary footbridge having come from Farlington (see photos 56 and 57).
(C.E.C. Townsend collection)

48. The unusual train formation, on 3rd May 1953, was for the Stephenson Locomotive Society's tour of Hampshire branch lines. The locomotive in the sandwich was class M7 no. 30110. (S.C. Nash)

London Brighton & South Coast Railway.

Arundel to

Hayling Island

47. Soon after the electrification of the coast line, a two-coach stopping train from Chichester over-ran the junction signals and collided with an express from Waterloo. (A.A.F. Bell collection)

49. Another unusual train was this ex-London Transport Central Line set. It is seen here on a driver training trip, prior to being shipped to the Isle of Wight later in 1967. The electric tramcar standing in the goods yard was bought by a group of enthusiasts who planned to electrify the Hayling branch, but the scheme was abortive. (S.C. Nash)

51. Only ¼ mile from Havant road bridge and only a few hundred yards from Bedhampton level crossing, Stockheath crossing was completely closed about 1970. The massive finial seems out of proportion to the main structure. (J. Scrace)

London Brighton & South Coast Railway.

Hayling Island to
Forest Hill

50. No. 47082 *Atlas* hauls the 10.20 (Saturdays only) train for Leeds via Oxford on 28th August 1982, the year in which this useful cross country service started. The frog in the down siding shows the location of the points until they were moved nearer to the platform in 1977. (J.S. Petley)

0248

BRITISH RAILWAYS (S)
This ticket is issued subject to the Bye-laws, Regulations and Conditions contained in the Publications and Notices of and applicable to the Railway Executive.

RAIL MOTOR CAR

Second Class
Fare 6d.
377-2

BETWEEN

North Hayling

and

HAYLING ISLAND

and RETURN

NOT
Transferable

JAN FEB MAR APR MAY JUN

JUL AUG SEP OCT NOV DEC

BEDHAMPTON

52. A turn-of-the-century tinted postcard of rural activity at this now busy urban location. Note the bi-directional signal.
(G. Knight collection)

54. Looking eastwards in 1973, we see the footbridge that was erected to replace Stockheath crossing. The Inspecting Officer in his report on the line before it opened in 1847 stated that *a bridge would be preferable . . . in view of the heavy traffic on the Turnpike Road!* The gates lasted until 1974 and the signal box until 1979. (J. Scrace)

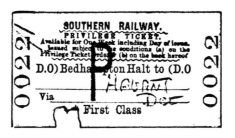

53. Looking westwards, we see the tiny booking office on the down platform in use. Similar facilities were provided on the up platform for many years. The timber decking was at last replaced in 1983. (Lens of Sutton)

55. Whilst the Turnpike Trustees failed to obtain a bridge, Bedhampton Parish Council persuaded the company to spend a massive £5000 on building an elaborate 21-arch double-curved bridge to carry a little used lane, which only went to the foreshore and a mill. This interesting structure still exists and can be seen in the background of this 1939 view of the Royal Train, which was hauled by class T9 no. 718. (C.R.L. Coles)

London Brighton & South Coast Railway.

Chelsea to

East Southsea

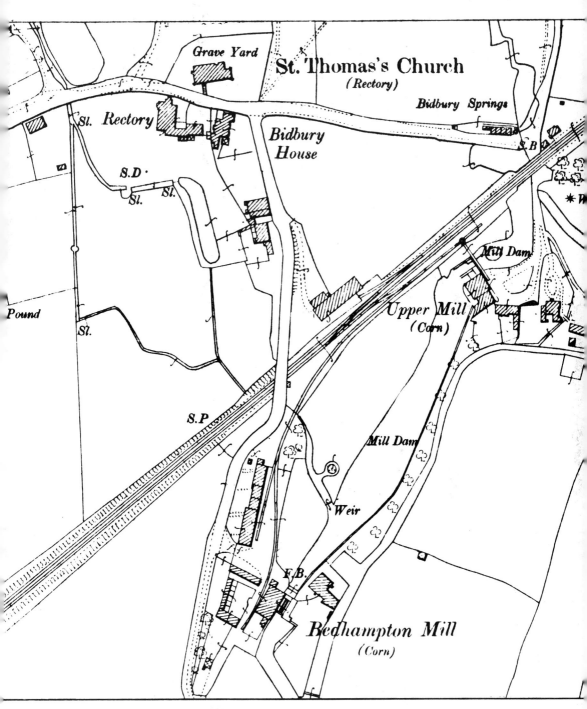

The 1897 map of 25" scale, shows a siding on the up side which is thought to have served a ship's biscuit factory. In later years, it terminated in a wagon turntable (still visible), from which a line ran north, to a granary. The Upper Mill siding was also used for supplying coal to the nearby Portsmouth Water Works until the early 1960s.

FARLINGTON

56. Looking west, on 23rd July 1894, we see the Portsmouth lines diverging to the left and the lines to Cosham on the right. The locomotive of a Fareham-bound train had traversed the junction successfully but the leading brake van was derailed and wrecked. The first coach turned over to the right; the second coach took to the up Portsmouth line and turned over to the left, whilst the remaining coaches piled up against the wreckage. The guard died and eight passengers were injured. (Lens of Sutton)

The 1897 map shows the racecourse station which was open on race days from 1891 and regularly from 1904 to 1917. The racecourse was not used again after World War I. (25" scale)

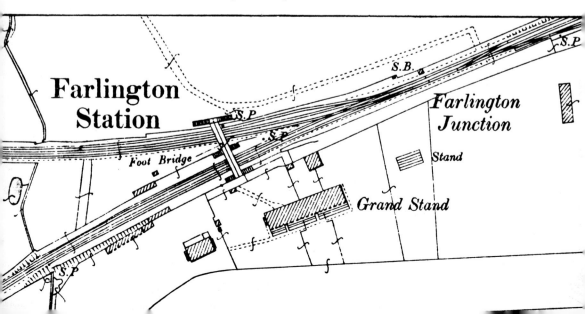

Farlington Station

Foot Bridge

S.B.

S.P.

S.P.

S.P.

Farlington Junction

Stand

Grand Stand

57. Class I3 4–4–2T no. 2083 sweeps round the curve en route for Portsmouth on 21st March 1936. The junction signal box can be seen in the distance. (H.C. Casserley)

The 1932 map shows the halt that was in use between 17th June 1928 and 4th July 1937.

SOUTHERN RAILWAY,
RAIL MOTOR CAR.
DAILY WORKMAN
Portsmouth Harbour
to
Farlington Halt
3rd Class Fare · 6d

FOR CONDITIONS
SEE BACK

SOUTHERN RAILWAY
RAIL MOTOR CAR.
DAILY WORKMAN
Farlington Halt
to
Portsmouth Harbour
3rd CLASS.
Passengers requested to see
tickets punched when issued.

0083

0083

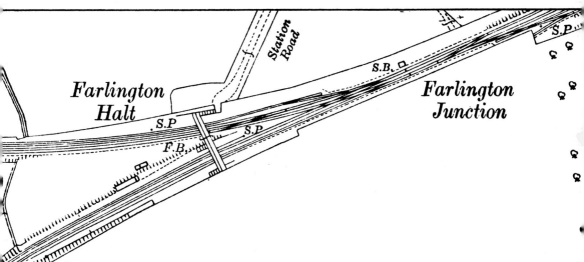

Farlington Halt

Farlington Junction

58. On the same day, we see an up train passing through, hauled by one of the "Greyhound" class T9, no. 282. The leading coach is a Maunsell 3rd-brake of 3-car set no. 225. (H.C. Casserley)

59. The rear coaches obscure sidings laid in 1948 for the Co-op Bakery. They ceased to be used at about the time this photograph was taken on 3rd November 1963. The junction signal box is behind the centre coach. In the foreground is the vestige of a siding that served an ammunition disposal area on the former racecourse site after World War I. The train is empty stock for an LCGB special to Hayling Island, on the day after passenger services had ceased on the branch. The locomotives are nos. 32670 (now *Bodiam* on the Kent & East Sussex Rly.) and 32636 (now *Fenchurch* on the Bluebell Rly.). (S.C. Nash)

60. This photograph of BR class 4 2–6–4T nos. 80139 was taken from the top of the once-fortified outer defences of Portsmouth, on 31st March 1967. The mixed livery coaches are passing over the defensive moat, across which drawbridges were originally provided. Behind the train is Port Creek, which separates the Portsmouth conurbation from the mainland. (J. Scrace)

61. The location of this box can be seen in the background of the previous photograph. It was closed on 5th May 1968, when Portsmouth Panel took over its functions. (J. Scrace)

62. These concrete "slab and harp" platforms were brought into use on 2nd November 1941, to serve nearby factories involved in essential war work. By the time T9 class no. 30288 was passing southwards in October 1955, many of the workers were departing by car and bicycle. For decades, only a few trains stopped in the rush hours but now the station is open all day. Admiralty sidings were located on the west side of the halt until recently. (P. Hay)

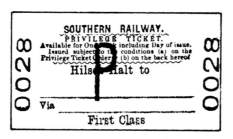

64. The gaswork's Peckett 0–4–0ST (no. 2100 of 1949) is seen in steam during a visit of the Ffestiniog Railway Hants & Sussex Area Group on 11th March 1967, shortly before the track was completely re-arranged for the reception of block trains of naptha tankers. The 1930 Aveling & Porter steam roller (OU 5979) was a temporary resident on the site, having worked most of its life in Eastleigh. Another of the gaswork's engines is illustrated in *Industrial Railways of the South East. (Middleton Press).* (M.J. Sheppard)

63. Life in the shadow of the gas holder was fairly uneventful until 26th August 1940, when an enemy bomb fell on the up side of the line but failed to explode. Passenger services were suspended but urgent supplies to the dockyard continued to pass by, with volunteer locomotive crews instructed to lie face down at this point. The box was photographed on 21st July 1976; reduced to a ground frame when the panel box opened and finally closed in November 1976.
(J. Scrace)

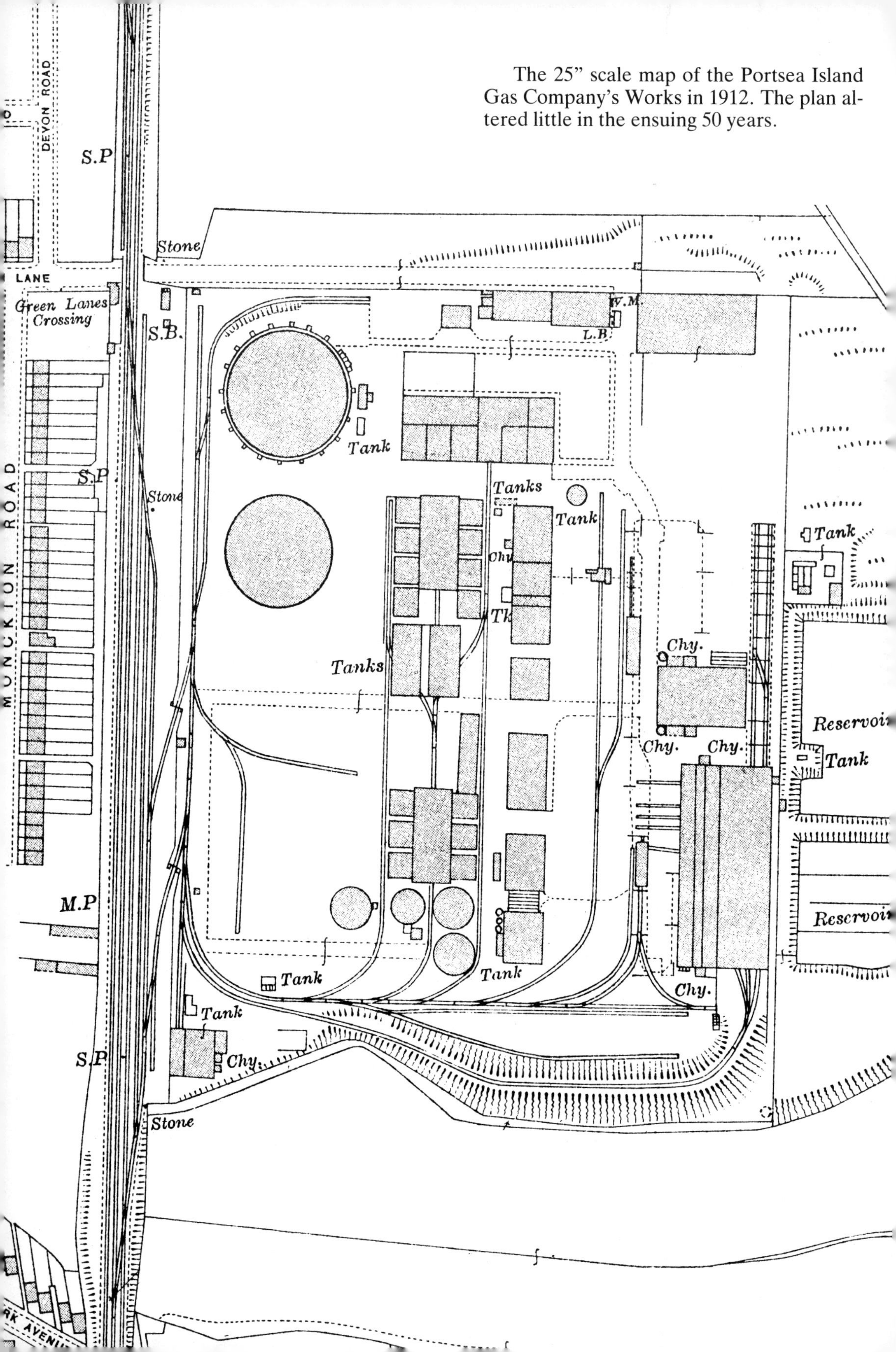

The 25" scale map of the Portsea Island Gas Company's Works in 1912. The plan altered little in the ensuing 50 years.

S.P

DEVON ROAD

GREEN ROAD

LANE

Green Lanes Crossing

S.B.

Stone

MONCKTON ROAD

S.P

Stone

Tank

Tanks

Tank

Chy

Tk

Tanks

Tanks

Tank

Tank

Chy.

Chy. Chy.

Reservoir

Tank

M.P

Tank

Tank

Chy.

Reservoir

Tank

Tank

Chy.

S.P

Tank

Chy.

Stone

RK AVENUE

Copnor Crossing Portsmouth

65. Plans for a station at Copnor were made in 1870 and again in 1879, but never materialised. This postcard shows Copnor crossing and signal box, which were both eliminated in 1935, and the railway cottage, which survives today. (Lens of Sutton)

London and South Western Rly.

From _____ HALWILL JUNO. 787

TO

Portsmouth Town

London Brighton & South Coast Railway.

Portsmouth to

Drayton

0049

SOUTHERN RAILWAY.
Restall's Half-Day Exe'n
Available as advertised.
Bournemouth Cen. to
WATERLOO
(Issued at London Bridge C.)
Third Class. Fare 8/-
FOR CONDITIONS
SEE BACK.

SOUTHERN RAILWAY.
Restall's Half-Day Exe'n
Available as advertised.
Waterloo to
PORTSMOUTH HAR.
thence by S.R. Coy's Steamer
to BOURNEMOUTH PIER
Including Pier Tolls
(Issued at London Bridge C.)
Third Class. Fare 8/-

0049

66. The station and the branch to Southsea were opened on 1st July 1885 and four years later a scheme was drawn up to use the large triangle of land between the main line and the branch for new locomotive sheds – one for each company! A northward view from the LBSCR shed towards the coal stage shows, from right to left, a Stroudley G class 2–2–2 no. 341 *Fairlight*, and two class C2 0–6–0 "Vulcans". (E.R. Lacey collection)

London and South Western Ry.

TO

787

FRATTON & SOUTHSEA

67. The junction signal box at the west end of the station lasted until 1968 but Terrier no. 48 only lasted until 1901. (A.A.F. Bell collection)

68. In the centre is the disused island platform of the former East Southsea branch; beyond the Great Western wagon is the junction signal box and behind the U class locomotive are the main line platforms. Photograph date – 28th October 1935. (H.C. Casserley)

69. The class I3 4–4–2T no. B27 was well suited to the relatively level route to Brighton and many of them were used on this duty until electrification. The roof of the branch platform is seen on the left, in the distance. (Lens of Sutton)

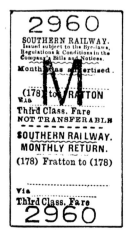

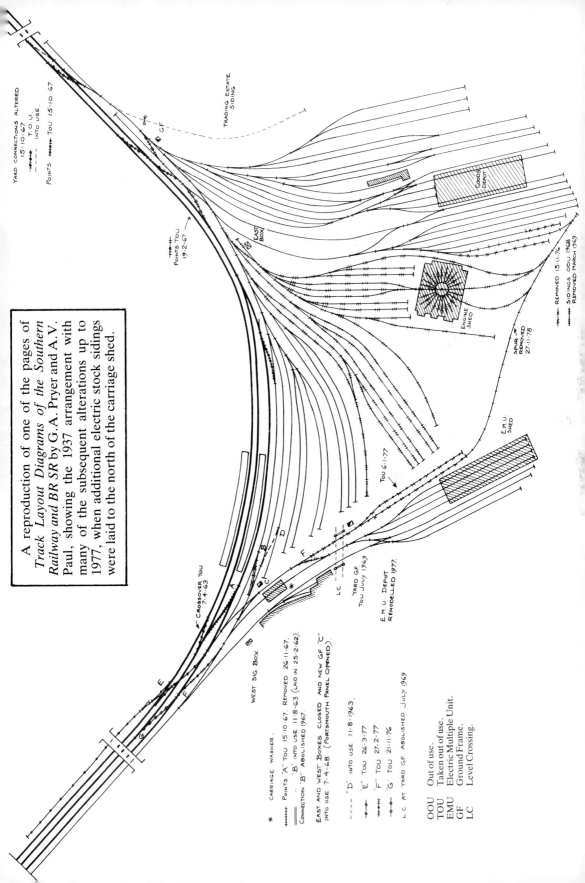

A reproduction of one of the pages of *Track Layout Diagrams of the Southern Railway and BR SR* by G. A. Pryer and A. V. Paul, showing the 1937 arrangement with many of the subsequent alterations up to 1977, when additional electric stock sidings were laid to the north of the carriage shed.

YARD CONNECTIONS ALTERED
15·10·67
T.O.U.
INTO USE.
POINTS ━━ TOU 15·10·67

TRADING ESTATE SIDING

GF

POINTS TOU 19·2·67

EAST BOX

GOODS DEPOT

ENGINE SHED

REMOVED 15·11·76
SIDINGS OOU 1968
REMOVED MARCH 1969

SPUR REMOVED 27·11·78

E.M.U. SHED

TOU 6·1·77

CROSSOVER TOU 7·4·63

A
B
C
D
F

LC

YARD GF TOU JULY 1969

E.M.U. DEPOT REMODELLED 1977.

G E
F

WEST SIG BOX

* CARRIAGE WASHER.

┿┿┿ POINTS "A" TOU 15·10·67 REMOVED 26·11·67.
━━━ "B" INTO USE 11·8·63 (LAID IN 25·2·62).
CONNECTION "B" ABOLISHED 1967.

EAST AND WEST BOXES CLOSED AND NEW GF "C"
INTO USE 7·4·68 (PORTSMOUTH PANEL OPENED).

---- "D" INTO USE 11·8·1963.

┿┿ "E" TOU 26·3·77
┿┿┿ "F" TOU 27·2·77
━━ "G" TOU 21·11·76

L.C. AT YARD GF ABOLISHED JULY 1969

OOU   Out of use.
TOU   Taken out of use.
EMU   Electric Multiple Unit.
GF   Ground Frame.
LC   Level Crossing.

70. Another view of devastation caused by the Nazi bombing of the locomotive shed on 11th January 1941 appears on the cover of the recently re-issued edition of *War on the Line (Middleton Press)*, the official history of the Southern Railway during WWII. Most of the engines were repaired within 14 days but ex-LSWR class T9 no. 118 (on the left) was out of action until 23rd May.
(National Railway Museum)

72. Steam serves steam. In 1956, coaling of locomotives was undertaken by steam crane. The receiving engine is E1 class 0–6–0T no. 32139 of 1879 vintage, designed by William Stroudley. (E. Gamblin)

71. When photographed by the East Box in June 1955, no. 30207 was Fratton's only O2. The size of this ancestor of today's containers was limited by the capacity of the average goods yard crane. They were known as the "suitcase of industry" and when retired, often became railway tool or equipment stores. (P. Hay)

73. The shed officially closed in November 1959 and the few remaining working engines stood outside. Inside on 25th July 1963 were some locomotives chosen for preservation. From right to left – "Terrier" no. 32662 (now at Bressingham), "Schools" no. 30925 *Cheltenham*, class M7 no. 30245, class N15 no. 30777 (the latter three now at the National Railway Museum, York) and no. 30850 *Lord Nelson* (now at Carnforth). The three former SR locomotives have been repainted in different versions of that company's livery. (J. Scrace)

74. On 25th June 1963, an unwelcome visitor from the Western Region arrived, with an excursion from Bristol. It was Castle class no. 5050, *Earl of St. Germans*. As it was too wide for the Southern Region loading gauge and its cylinders had grazed the platform at Fareham, it was impounded behind two Q1s until a plan for its safe return could be prepared. (B.R. Oliver)

75. The carriage washing plant was erected on the site of the branch platform in 1937. Here we see Q class no. 30548 creeping forward with a smart set of Bulleid coaches forming the LCGB Hampshire Venturer Rail Tour on 18th April 1964. (S.C. Nash)

76. These massive gates, photographed in 1968, were originally provided to protect the roadway into the goods yard, where it crossed the Southsea branch. The crossing remained in use until 1969, although the lines were only carriage sidings. The signal box was of LSWR design. (J. Scrace)

77. A stopping service to Waterloo arrives, whilst a class 33 diesel locomotive enters the quadruple track section to Portsmouth & Southsea, on its way to the Harbour station where its coaches (for Bristol or Cardiff) will be standing. (J. Scrace)

78. No. 33027 *Earl Mountbatten of Burma* stands in the fuelling road in October 1980. No steam cranes. No ash pits. No turntables. Progress indeed. Note the snow ploughs, often needed when crossing Salisbury Plain on the Bristol run. (J. Scrace)

EAST SOUTHSEA BRANCH

79. "Terrier" no. 48 *Leadenhall*, with a LBSCR train of Stroudley designed 4-wheeled coaches, stands at the branch platform, in the 1890s. The station was officially named Fratton & Southsea between 1905 and 1921. Half the services were worked by the LSWR, usually hauled by a class O2 0–4–4 tank. (E.R. Lacey collection)

80. The branch was a costly white elephant and means of reducing operating costs were sought by the Joint Committee. They arranged for steam railcars to be built at Eastleigh in 1903, no. 1 being painted LBSCR chocolate and cream and no. 2 being finished in LSWR green. They were a dismal failure and within months they were both rebuilt with small horizontal boilers and larger diameter cylinders. (Portsmouth City Council Archives)

The 1896 6" scale map showing the entire length of the 1¼ mile branch, part of which was still running through fields at that time. The quadruple track between the two main line stations was laid on the route of the former Portsmouth and Arundel Canal.

81. After rebuilding, they were prone to regular mechanical failure and when full of passengers, often needed a banking engine to assist. The two saloons seated 30 passengers, third class, and 12 passengers, first class. The vestibules had curious iron trellis gates, similar to those on the Waterloo & City line. (Lens of Sutton)

EAST SOUTHSEA,

Fares—1st, 12/4 ; 2nd, 7/9 ; 3rd, 6/2. Return—1st, 21/6 ; 2nd, 13/6 ; 3rd, 11/8.

45¼ miles from Brighton, and 78 from Tunbridge Wells. About the middle of the present century the wide tract of shore bordering the Solent in the neighbourhood of Southsea Castle was selected as a site for the erection of some high-class marine residences. In the course of a few years these villas proved a nucleus for the large, fashionable, and high-class watering-place of Southsea, which not only annually attracts a considerable number of wealthy visitors, but has become a favourite place of residence with many of the naval and military officers attached to the extensive establishments of the United Services in Portsmouth and its vicinity. Amongst its most noteworthy buildings are numerous good hotels and superior boarding establishments receiving guests *en pension*. Such an exceptional combination of advantages, alike for residents or visitors, has caused the season—from June to October—to become noted for its attractions. One of the most-frequented resorts is the Clarence Esplanade Pier, provided with reading-rooms and a highly ornamental concert pavilion, in which popular concerts are held on Monday evenings, a military band also performing twice daily.

82. When the line was singled in 1904, two halts were built close to road bridges in an attempt to win traffic for the branch. This is Jessie Road bridge, with the path to the halt on the extreme right. (British Rail)

L. & S. W. & L. B. & S. C. Joint Rly.
This Ticket is issued subject to the Regulations and Conditions stated in the joint Companies Time Tables and Bills.

(S.2)
EAST SOUTHSEA to FRATTON.

Available on day of issue only.
To be shown on demand.

Fare for single journey
FIRST CLASS 2d.

FRATTON AND SOUTHSEA and EAST SOUTHSEA (Motor Cars—1st and 3rd class).—L. & S. W. and L. B. & S. C.—1½ miles.
Fratton and Southsea to East Southsea every 20 minutes from 8 mrn. to 7 20 aft., calling at Jessie Road Bridge and Albert Road Bridge.
East Southsea to Fratton and Southsea every 20 minutes from 8 10 mrn. to 7 30 aft., calling at Albert Road Bridge and Jessie Road Bridge.
☞ Cars connect at Fratton with the Principal Trains to and from London, Southampton, Basingstoke, Salisbury, Winchester, Chichester, Arundel, Brighton, &c

(Bradshaw 1910)

83. The two photographs were taken in 1913 as engineering records of the bridge ramps – hence the curious composition which frustratingly only shows part of a Portsmouth Corporation tram. The nameboard of Albert Road Halt is below Pickford's advertisement. Both bridges disappeared after the track was lifted in 1925-26. (British Rail)

84. The hopelessly extravagant terminus had three platforms which matched the exuberant local architecture. The driver of this "Terrier" had no intention of running short of coal on the branch and his wooden brake blocks would also last him for some time yet. (Lens of Sutton)

FRATTON and SOUTHSEA.—London and South Western and London, Brighton, and South Coast.
Fratton ....dep 7 25 8 0 8 25 8 55 9 19 9 40 10 2 1043 1110 1140 12 3 1 7 1 30 2 15 2 35 3 2 3 26 4 23 5 26 5 45 6 36 7 10 7 36 ....
Southsea ......arr 7 31 8 5 8 31 9 1 9 25 9 46 10 8 1054 1116 1145 12 8 1 13 1 35 2 21 2 40 3 8 3 32 4 29 5 32 5 50 6 42 7 15 7 42 ....
Southsea 52,68 dp 7 0 7 50 8 11 8 45 9 10 9 30 9 50 1030 1058 1130 1155 1212 1 20 1 50 2 25 2 50 3 15 4 10 4 40 5 35 6 15 7 0 7 20 ....
Fratton 53,47,70, 7 6 7 55 8 17 8 51 9 16 9 36 9 56 1036 11 4 1135 12 0 1218 1 26 1 55 2 30 2 56 3 21 4 15 4 46 5 40 6 21 7 6 7 25 ....

(Bradshaw 1890)

85. As a further economy measure in 1904, the main station buildings were leased out and were used by motor engineers for many years. A small covered platform for the rail-motor service was erected and is seen on the right of this Edwardian view. The terminus acquired the prefix "East" in 1896. (C. Fry collection)

PORTSMOUTH & SOUTHSEA

86. The present name was used between 1861 and 1876 and again from 1921. In the interval it was appropriately – "Portsmouth Town". The handsome exterior of the 1866 terminal buildings, viewed from the high level platforms, was, until recently, obscured by overgrown lime trees. (Lens of Sutton)

87. The vaulted concourse roof with stylish elliptical arches remains to be enjoyed today. Today's lighting is more functional but less attractive than yesterday's gas lanterns. (Lens of Sutton)

88. Unfortunately the date of this photograph of the station staff outside the present parcels office has not survived the passage of time. (National Railway Museum)

89. The notes on the back of this photograph state that it was taken in 1869. No. 253 had been built in the previous year by Slaughter & Co. of Bristol to Craven's design and was scrapped in 1896. (E.R. Lacey collection)

90. An eastward view, taken circa 1930, with a train about to depart from the station's shortest platform, no. 1. The fish dock is on the far left and a fine selection of vehicles is on show for the rolling stock historian. (Lens of Sutton)

91. LSWR "Jubilee" class A12 0–4–2 no. 622 waits to leave platform 5. In the distance is the substantial footbridge known as Jacobs Ladder which is one of the the few features of this photograph still standing today. (Lens of Sutton)

92. Former LSWR class K10 no. 388 stands in no. 2 platform, circa 1935. Many railway photographs have been ruined by excess steam. Here it adds atmosphere, as only one buffer has been lost to view. (C.R.L. Coles)

93. Viewed from the north end of Jacobs Ladder, we see the locomotive servicing and turning facilities, which were retained until 1967. On the turntable road is Southern Railway no. 429 of class L12. The site is now occupied by the panel box. (E. Jackson)

94. The palatial goods shed was on the south side of the high level platforms and was closed in 1936 to make way for sidings for the impending electric trains. Note the 3-wheeled mechanical horse in the centre. (E. Jackson)

95. Much of the fine ornamental detail of this part of the building survived the Blitz. The recent restoration and conservation programme will do much to preserve this facade for future admirers. (E. Jackson)

→

97. No. 5 is the longest of the low level platforms and was often used for the Cardiff trains. On the left is the 1 in 61 gradient that is necessary to carry the Harbour lines and high level platforms over Commercial Road. Platforms 4 and 5 are likely to be the only low level ones to be retained if the current redevelopment plan goes ahead.
(Lens of Sutton)

96. Photographed on 27th April 1941, we witness the bomb damage suffered by the north end of the building, along with vast areas of hard-hit Portsmouth. This area is now partly occupied by British Transport Police. (British Rail)

PORTSMOUTH YARD

98. A closer look at the massive signal box, again from Jacobs Ladder. Note the impressive return flight of steps. It was superseded by the panel box in 1968. (D. Cullum)

LONDON, BRIGHTON, & SOUTH-COAST RAILWAY

FARES BETWEEN BRIGHTON AND PORTSMOUTH,

AND THE IMTERMEDIATE STATIONS.

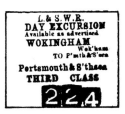

DAY TICKETS.				BRIGHTON TO	BY ORDINARY TRAINS.				
1st Class.		2nd Class.			Distance	1st Class.	2nd Class.	3rd Class.	Parliamentary.
s.	d.	s.	d.		Miles.	s. d.	s. d.	s. d	s. d.
1	9	1	4	Hove Station......	1	1 0	0 9	0 6	0 1
1	9	1	4	Southwick	4½	1 0	0 9	0 6	0 5
1	9	1	4	Kingston	5⅛	1 0	0 9	0 6	0 5
1	9	1	4	Shoreham	5¾	1 0	0 9	0 6	0 5
3	0	2	0	Lancing	8¼	1 8	1 3	0 10	0 8
2	6	1	9	Worthing	10½	2 0	1 6	1 0	0 10
3	0	2	4	Goring	13⅛	2 9	2 0	1 4	1 1
4	0	3	0	Angmering	15½	3 3	2 4	1 7	1 3
5	0	3	9	Littlehampton	17	3 9	2 10	1 10	1 5
5	0	3	9	Arundel	19½	4 0	3 0	2 0	1 7
5	6	4	0	Yapton	20	4 5	3 4	2 2	1 8
6	0	4	6	Bognor	23½	5 0	3 9	2 6	1 11
7	0	5	6	Drayton	26½	5 6	4 2	2 9	2 2
7	6	6	0	Chichester	28½	6 0	4 6	3 0	2 4
8	0	6	6	Bosham	31½	6 6	4 10	3 3	2 7
8	6	7	0	Emsworth	35½	7 4	5 6	3 8	2 11
8	6	7	0	Havant	37⅛	7 10	5 10	3 11	3 1
10	6	8	0	Portsmouth	44½	9 4	7 0	4 8	3 8

→

100. The signal box was reduced to ground frame status in 1930, and the line was closed in 1978. The severity of the gradient is clearly seen in this 1968 photograph but no trace of this embankment remains today. (J. Scrace)

99. The intimate nature of the high level train sheds needs to be experienced, not read about. The limited clearances, the total enclosure and the tremendous vibration are impressive. On the left, on 6th August 1983, is a Salisbury-bound DEMU and, on the right, two full length carriage sidings and a short one, for 4 cars. The initials of the Joint Extension Railway are cast into many of the canopy stanchion brackets. (V. Mitchell)

101. Half way along platform 6, a branch diverged away sharply to the North Dock-yard. Prior to 1876, it crossed the street on the level. On the left is the former Post Office building. Class 33 no. D6543 is seen on 9th January 1969. It was later renumbered 33025. (J. Scrace)

102. There were two level crossings over public highways. The first one was over Edinburgh Road, and the distinctive Admiralty gates are still in place. Here we see class 02 no. 3027 on its way to the Dockyard on 18th September 1953. (Pamlin Prints)

103. The same locomotive returns from the Dockyard but was photographed nearly two years later. The post of the antique bi-directional signal was subsequently replaced by a lattice one which is still in situ today. (P. Hay)

104. An August 1969 view of the last steam
locomotive in the Dockyard. It is no. 17,
built in 1938 by Andrew Barclay, works
no. 2051. (R.D. Smith)

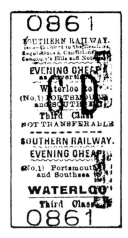

105. To reduce light engine running to
Fratton for turning, a turntable was pro-
vided, until 1946, between Portsmouth &
Southsea and Portsmouth Harbour, near
Burnaby Road bridge. LBSCR class E5
no. 576 *Brenchley* stands amid heaps of
clinker and facing the Guildhall.
(Lens of Sutton)

London Brighton & South Coast Railway.

Chelsea to

Portsmouth Town

106. The 1876 track layout proved inadequate and was widened, as shown in the next picture. The LBSCR slotted post signals have the rotating type of shunt signal. No. 212 *Armstrong* is of class B2. (E.R. Lacey collection)

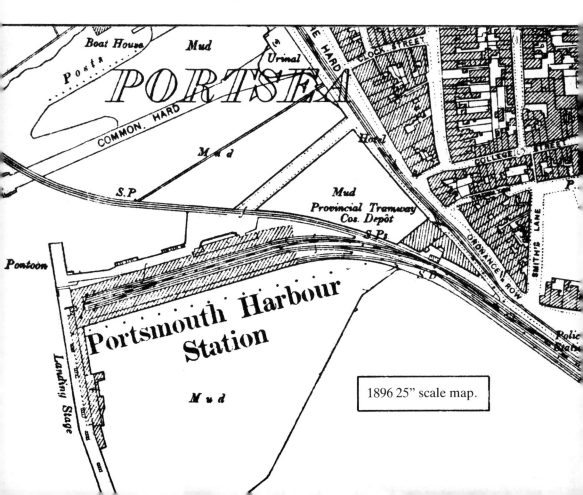

1896 25" scale map.

107. The shunt signals were changed to the LSWR type and an additional lattice post was erected for the new platforms. The line on the extreme right descended to the Gun Wharf. It was used intermittently until 1930 and again from 1937. (Lens of Sutton)

108. The Isle of Wight ferry berth in Queen Victoria's day displayed some fine cast iron tracery, ornate gas lamps and a steam crane. In the distance is the Dockyard Signal Tower. (National Railway Museum)

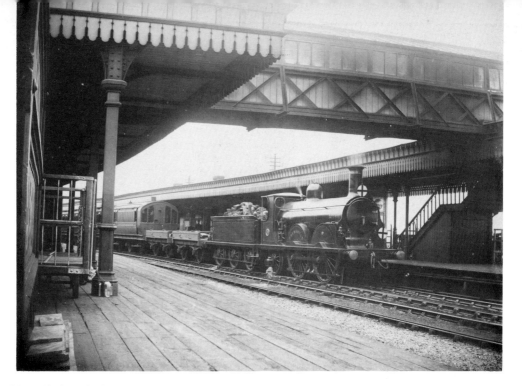

109. All the platforms were built over the inter-tidal area – hence the wooden decking. "Gladstone" class no. 193 *Fremantle* , built in 1888, is seen coupled to flat wagons of the type used for conveying the horse-drawn carriages of the wealthy. A less serious aspect of an accident involving this locomotive at Wivelsfield in 1899, was the trapping of a gentleman's beard in a sliding door. The breakdown gang was called for, in preference to a sharp knife. (E.R. Lacey collection)

110. D1 class no. 239 was built in 1881 and lasted until 1948. Behind its bunker is one of the trolleys used for Isle of Wight traffic. The lifting eyes were provided for them to be craned into the ferry holds. During WWII this loco was fitted with a fire pump and allocated to Hither Green marshalling yard, in south-east London. (E.R. Lacey collection)

LONDON BRIGHTON AND SOUTH COAST RAILWAY.

TIME TABLE OF THE SPECIAL TRAIN

CONVEYING

HIS MAJESTY

KING EDWARD VII.

AND SUITE,

FROM

PORTSMOUTH DOCKYARD TO VICTORIA,

On MONDAY, FEBRUARY 12th, 1906.

TIME TABLE.		P.M.			TIME TABLE.		P.M.		
		arr.	pass.	dep.			arr.	pass.	dep.
PORTSMOUTH DOCKYARD	...	...		**2 40**	Pulborough				3 31
(South Railway Jetty)					Billingshurst				3 37
Portsmouth Harbour Signal Box	...	2 42		2 43	Horsham				3 46
(to take up Pilotman)					**Warnham**				3 49
Portsmouth Town (High Level)				2 45	Ockley				3 54
Fratton				2 46	Holmwood				3 57
Havant				2 55	Dorking				4 4
Emsworth				2 57	Leatherhead				4 9
Bosham				3 2	Epsom Town				4 14
Chichester				3 7	Sutton				4 20
Barnham				3 14	Mitcham Junction				4 25
Ford				3 18	Balham				4 30
Arundel				3 22	Clapham Junction				4 34
Amberley				3 26	VICTORIA STATION		**4 40**		...

LONDON BRIDGE STATION,
10th February, 1906.

WILLIAM FORBES,
General Manager.

111. The South Dockyard branch curved north-westwards from the Harbour station signal box. As it cut off the foreshore from the harbour a 40ft. swing bridge had to be provided. South Railway Jetty had an elaborate waiting shelter for important passengers but never had a public passenger service. Harbour station is in the background, with a Gosport ferry on the right. The locomotive is class B4 no. 42 *His Majesty*, of 1902. (E. Jackson collection)

112. The steam crane seen in photograph no. 108 was just one victim of the devastation that was to be seen on 22nd August 1940. Worse was to come. (British Rail)

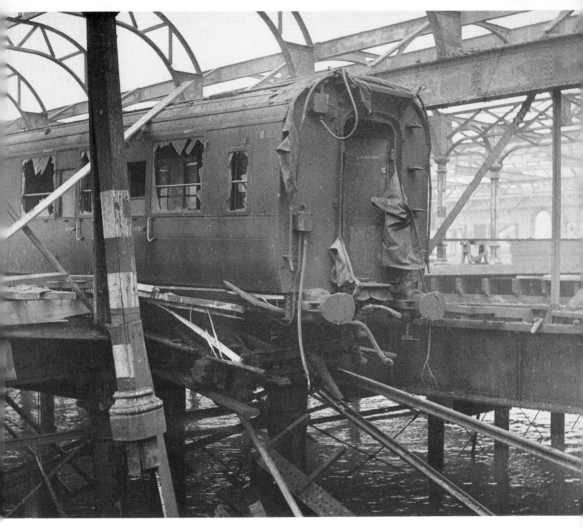

113. On 10th January 1941, the destruction was almost complete. The wooden platforms burnt uncontrollably. Set no. 3132 was wrecked. The signal box was totally destroyed. The station was effectively closed until 1st June 1946, although one platform could be used to accommodate nine coaches only. (British Rail)

London Brighton & South Coast Railway.

Horeham Road to

Portsmouth Har.

114. The post-war holiday boom brought almost unmanageable crowds to the station. On the left a train from London (one of the electric set nick-named "Nelsons" or "Pompeys") and on the right a train from South Wales (headed by *Raveningham Hall*, now preserved on the Severn Valley Railway). (Lens of Sutton)

115. The passenger concourse between the platform ends and the ferry berth was almost completely rebuilt in 1945-6. Electric trolley cranes were provided but nowadays most parcel traffic to the Island goes direct by road vehicles on the car ferries. (Lens of Sutton)

116. The Fratton 02 no. 30207, seen earlier in picture no. 71, was handling a heavy load of empty coaches for a Saturday Extra, when photographed in June 1955. Trains for the Gun Wharf had formerly descended between the two walls; reversed and proceeded along the track in the foreground. (P. Hay)

117. The 1946 signal box was rendered obsolete in 1968 but the building has been retained for other purposes. The upper floor serves as a mess room for permanent way workers and the lower part is used as a remote relay room. (J. Scrace)

118. A train of 2 BIL units makes up a fast train from Brighton, at the approach to the terminus on 30th July 1970. Another view of the former incline to the Gun Wharf is obtained on the right. Also on the right is the no. 5 platform road, off which there is a short siding used for oil tankers supplying fuel for the ferries. (J. Scrace)

119. The Paddle Steamer *Portsdown*, built at Dundee in 1928, was one of a number of railway owned vessels requisitioned to assist in the evacuation of Dunkirk. It came into the news again, when it hit a mine, whilst operating the 4.00 am service to Ryde, on 20th September 1941. Twenty died and seventeen were saved. (E. Jackson collection)

120. The Motor Vessel *Brading* (photographed here in 1973) and its sister ship *Southsea* were introduced in 1948, after which the paddle steamers were gradually withdrawn. The Ryde route has been operated or controlled by the railways for most of its history. This year, Sealink has been acquired by Sea Containers Ltd and the present ageing vessels will no doubt be replaced in the near future. This company already has a good railway connection, as owners of the Venice Simplon-Orient-Express. (E. Wilmshurst)

APRIL AND MAY, 1913.

SEA TRIPS FROM PORTSMOUTH

(Weather and other circumstances permitting).

SUNDAYS AND MONDAYS IN APRIL, AND EVERY WEEK-DAY AND SUNDAY IN MAY.

TO RYDE.

ON MONDAYS IN APRIL, AND EVERY WEEK-DAY IN MAY Return Tickets will be issued from Portsmouth Harbour by 11.25 a.m. and Southsea Pier by the 11.35 a.m. and subsequent Boats (also from Portsmouth Town and from Fratton in May).

Every SUNDAY Return Tickets will be issued from Portsmouth Harbour and Southsea Piers by any Boat (also from Portsmouth Town after 11.0 a.m. in May). Returning from Ryde the same day by any Boat.

Fares (including Pier Dues) from Portsmouth Harbour and Southsea Piers: First Class, 1s. 6d. Second Class, 1s. 2d. From Portsmouth Town Station: First Class, 1s. 10d.; Third Class, 1s. 4d. From Fratton, First Class, 2s.; Third Class, 1s. 5d.

TO THE ISLE OF WIGHT (Via RYDE).

FROM	To any Station on the Isle of Wight, or Isle of Wight Central Railway (including Bembridge, St. Helens, Godshill, Whitwell, St. Lawrence, and Ventnor Town).		Return Fares, including all Pier Tolls.	
	On Mondays only in April, and every Week-day in May.	SUNDAYS.	1st Class.	3rd Class
Portsmouth Harbour	By all Boats† up to 3.40 p.m. (4.0 p.m. on Saturdays only.)	By all Boats up to 2.10 p.m. (New Ventnor line excepted).	3/6	2/6
Southsea Pier ...	By all Boats† up to 3.50 p.m. (4.10 p.m. on Saturdays only).	By all Boats up to 2.20 p.m. (New Ventnor line excepted).	3/6	2/6

† Last Boat to New Ventnor Line 1.55 p.m. from Portsmouth Harbour, and 1.25 p.m. from Southsea Pier.
The Joint Railway Companies do not guarantee the connection between their Boats and the Trains in either direction.

Other Books from Middleton Press

BRANCH LINE SERIES
Vic Mitchell and Keith Smith
BRANCH LINES TO MIDHURST
BRANCH LINES TO HORSHAM
BRANCH LINE TO SELSEY
BRANCH LINES TO EAST GRINSTEAD
BRANCH LINES TO ALTON
BRANCH LINE TO HAYLING
BRANCH LINE TO SOUTHWOLD

SOUTH COAST RAILWAY SERIES
Vic Mitchell and Keith Smith
BRIGHTON TO WORTHING
WORTHING TO CHICHESTER

OTHER BOOKS
INDUSTRIAL RAILWAYS OF THE SOUTH-EAST
Chalk Pits Museum
GREEN ROOF OF SUSSEX
Charles Moore
MIDHURST TOWN – THEN AND NOW
Vic and Barbara Mitchell
STEAMING THROUGH KENT
Peter Hay